RISE AGAIN

Minister Jessie "J.C." Daniels

Copyright © 2012 by Jessie Daniels

Published by J.C. Books

For publishing information

J.C. Books
304 Riverwood Dr.
Louisburg, NC 27549
jcdaniels54@yahoo.com

All rights reserved, including the right of reproduction
in whole or in part in any form.

No part of this publication may be stored in any retrieval system or transmitted in any form or by electronic, mechanical, photocopying, recording or otherwise without the written permission of the publisher except the case of brief quotations embodied in critical articles and reviews.

Printed in the
United States of America

ISBN-13: 978-1475085983

ISBN-10:1475085982

Dedication

I give honor to my Lord and Savior Jesus Christ, who inspired me to write this book. To my wife, whom I led to Jesus Christ, it has been such a joy to watch you evolve into the Woman of God that you are today. You are more beautiful today than when we first met over 33 years ago. I did not know when I married you how much of a treasure I was actually getting; but you are truly a diamond. You are my queen! Every year I walk with God, He helps me to improve. He is making a good husband and father out of me. I am anointed to be your man for such a time as this. It is because of your vote of confidence in me, I believe that the sky is the limit, and I will fulfill the assignment that God has placed on my life.

Acknowledgements

There are a number of wonderful people who contributed in countless ways to my experiences in writing this book. My gratitude to my children, the late Rev. D.Doc Taylor, Jermaine Jones, Tameka Jones, Terrell Daniels, Donnie Daniels and Franchesta Davis. My sisters, Josette Daniels, Mrs. Judie D. Barnes, and Jill C. Daniels. Other family members, aunts, uncles, nieces, nephews, cousins, and in-laws. I will always appreciate your love and support. I also want to acknowledge the compassion and encouragement of my church family, Freedom and Deliverance Outreach Center, Louisburg, NC, especially my Bishop and Pastor Lorenzo N. Peterson, Sr., whom God used to confirm to me that it was time to step out and do it. I want to especially thank my Aunt Ida Mae Hicks of Buffalo, NY, my Aunt Annie L. Tyson-Hubbard of Greenville NC. My uncles, Joe Louis Daniels of Scotland Neck, and William M. Daniels (Pardner) of Baltimore MD, because they continued to encourage me to be the best that I can be, in spite of my past, plus they let me know they were proud of the change I had made in my life! I was greatly inspired to write this book after seeing how the Lord Jesus Christ had changed the lives of my sister Josette Daniels, and my cousin Lorie Tyson Savage, who were also on drugs, but today they are living productive and successful lives, and making a difference in the lives of others. And thank you to Brother Bruce and Sister Tiana Davis of Around HIM Publishing. Special thanks to Brother Bobby and Sister Lola Thompson.

In the midst of this book being completed, the Lord had led my wife and me to New Hope Worship Center in Louisburg, NC, where the Pastor is Joe Ferguson.

Table of Contents

Foreword..8
Preface..9
Chapter 1
   WHERE IT ALL BEGAN..11
Chapter 2
   MY HIGH SCHOOL YEARS...13
Chapter 3
   MY COLLEGE DAYS...15
Chapter 4
   MY PROFESSIONAL BASEBALL DAYS.....................17
Chapter 5
   COMING BACK HOME..20
Chapter 6
   LIFE AFTER BASEBALL...22
Chapter 7
   MY FIRST RELEASE..29
Chapter 8
   IT'S OVER...32
Chapter 9
   SAYING GOODBYE..35
Chapter 10
   JANET TAKES ME BACK...37
Chapter 11
   MY SECOND MARRIAGE...39
Chapter 12
   MY LAST TIME IN PRISON...41
Chapter 13
   DEVOTIONS...47
   PRIORITES....(I ASKED GOD).....................................49
Chapter 14
   TRANSFORMATION...52
Chapter 15
   LIFE AFTER BUNN...54

WASTED TIME..58
J.C.'S QUOTATIONS...60
WORDS OF
INSPIRATION AND ENCOURAGEMENT...61
FINAL THOUGHTS..62
IN MEMORY OF..63
REFLECTIONS OF ME..65

Rise Again

Foreword

It is wonderful to see God change hearts and lives. I have had the privilege of hearing, knowing and seeing what the Lord has done in the life of my good friend and brother Jessie Daniels. Jessie and I met in 2006 here at New Hope Worship Center on the basketball court. We bonded together because of the kindred spirit we both had in the Lord. As we spent time together, it was apparent the Lord had brought him out of many strongholds and set him free by the spirit of the Lord. We rejoice together because of the witness my brother is to this hurting world. Jessie not only talks the talk but walks the walk. Brother Jessie became a member here at New Hope Worship Center in 2010 and has ministered to many. He has preached on several occasions and taught small groups. I love him and his dear wife Lois and they are a blessing to many in this church and community. May God use this book Rise Again to bless many more people who need the transforming grace of Jesus Christ to change their lives!

God Bless!

Pastor Joe Ferguson
New Hope Worship Center
PO Box 430
Bunn, NC 27508

Preface

Rise Again was born in my heart in the summer of 2005 while being in prison for the 3rd. time. I asked God, "Where do I go from here?" He placed it upon my heart that He had great things in store for me, and I needed to write a book about my life story. To teach others that winners in life are not those who never stumble in life, but they are the ones capable of rising up one more time than they fall down. Then, after overcoming failure, they run with new strength and soar with wings like an eagle, above the turmoil and confusion in life. Let others know that failure is never final for those who begin again with God. Failure is a fact of life, but not a way of life. People must realize that even the failed choices and wrong turns in life can be redeemed by God, if you are willing to let Him. We all must come to the realization that we were created for a God-given purpose. My main objective is to let people know that no matter where you are in life, today, that God loves you, He still cares for you and He can still use you for His Glory!

When writing this book, I had to pour out my heart as I shared the many painful experiences I suffered as a result of my drug addiction. My desire is for those who read it to be provoked, encouraged and inspired to overcome. Remember what Jesus said in Mark 9:23 (NKJ); "If you can believe. All things are possible to him that believes."

I hope that this book will be a blessing to all who read it!

Chapter 1

WHERE IT ALL BEGAN

My nickname is J.C. which was given to me by my late grandmother, Mrs. Magnolia Cooper Daniels. I was born on Nov. 7, 1954, to the late Mr. Jessie Lee Daniels, Jr., and the late Mrs. Erma Teel Daniels, in Greenville, NC. I am the oldest of 5 children, 2 boys and 3 girls. My only brother and best friend, Jeffrey M. Daniels, died on Nov. 20, 2006, from a brain tumor, and I miss him dearly. My three sisters, Josette L. Daniels, Mrs. Judie D. Barnes, and Jill C. Daniels, are the loveliest sisters a brother could have. I was 5 years old when my parents moved into a new subdivision called Greenfield Terrace in 1960. This was an upscale middle class neighborhood. It was a community of mostly preachers, teachers, policemen, and a few other hard-working people. This is where I developed my skills to become one of the best athletes ever to come out of Greenville. A lot of people still think of me as a baseball legend, calling me the best baseball player ever to come out Greenville, NC. I attended St. Gabriel's Catholic School, grades 1-8, graduating with honors in June of 1968, as valedictorian, with a 95.3 grade point average. I memorized the late Dr. Martin Luther King Jr.'s I Have a Dream speech, and I spoke it as my graduation speech. I was 9 years old when I began to participate in organized sports. I played rec. league football, basketball, and baseball, at the South Greenville Recreation Center. To be honest, I was pretty good in all 3 sports, but I was a natural baseball player. A strange thing happened to me when I was 12 years old. I began to have aspirations of being a Catholic Priest. I was an altar boy at St. Gabriel's Catholic Church, serving Mass at the time, and I felt good about serving God at a young age. It felt like it was what I was supposed to be doing. But the priest told me that you could not be involved with females in an intimate way, or get married, so I knew I had to change my thoughts about this, because I really liked girls. So I soon put my mind back on playing sports. I graduated from the Little Leagues in baseball when I turned 13 years old. In April 1968, my father took my best child-hood friend, Larry Earl Dixon, and me over to Guy Smith Stadium, to try out for the all-white Babe Ruth League in Greenville, ages 13-15. We were the first African Americans to integrate the Babe Ruth league. You see, my father was a civil rights activist, who believed in equality for all and that is why he took us over to play in the white leagues because they had the best coaches and playing facilities at that time. My father was a man of integrity, a stand up type man, who was no nonsense. He was blessed to have marched and demonstrated in Washington, DC with the late, great Dr. Martin Luther King Jr., in 1963 during the famous march on Washington, and again with Dr. King in Edenton, NC, in 1965. He definitely believed that all men are created equal and when there was injustice done to blacks, he was one of the first ones on the scene to find out why, and help find a solution to the problem. In fact, he was my hero growing up!

My mother was a very sweet, loving, and kind Christian woman who would give a stranger the clothes off her back to help them. She was an evangelist, who would later become a pastor. My mother possessed a Hannah type spirit, because she was always praying, and praising God. She was the one who prayed for our family that we would all be saved. God answered her prayers, even though she passed away before she had a chance to see it come to pass. She always stood on the word of God, that he would save her entire household. In fact, all of her children; have gotten saved and my father was saved and baptized before he passed away February, 1995. My mother's favorite scripture was Joshua 24:15 "Choose ye this day whom you will serve, but as for me and my house, we will serve the Lord!" Hallelujah!

Chapter 2

MY HIGH SCHOOL YEARS

In September, 1968, I was one of 30 blacks to attend the predominately white J. H. Rose High School in Greenville, NC. The population of the high school was 1,650, so you could imagine what we had to go through, the name calling, pictures of blacks being lynched and other forms of prejudice. By the time I was 15, I was the MVP of my baseball team, Carolina Dairies. I was picked for the all-star team. I led the 14-15 year old all-stars to the state championship in Kings Mountain, NC. We were the regional runner-up in Huntsville, Alabama, in the summer of 1970. I was 10-0 as a pitcher, a .415 batter, with about 10 home runs, and 30 stolen bases. During this time, I learned that I had potential to become a professional baseball player one day. In fact, a scout from the Cincinnati Reds major league team, talked with my father about staying in contact with me to keep up with my progress in baseball while I was in high school. At the age of 16, my junior year of high school, I began to concentrate on 2 sports: basketball and baseball. I was selected to the 4-A high school All –Conference and All State Team in 1971. I was named as one of the best 25 high school baseball players in America, by the Greensboro Daily Record, that same year. I was also named to the All State Baseball Team by the Greensboro Daily Record, my senior year, and the New York Mets wanted to sign me to a professional baseball contract, but I got into trouble. My best friend Larry got into a fight with a white student who was a 6 ft. 6 in. tall, 230lbs. football player. When I came to Larry's rescue, the white boy's parents took out a warrant on us for assault. This was cool with us because we knew that it would be a long time before he messed with another black person. This incident just so happened to be right before our final exams and a few weeks before graduation. We were suspended for 3 days and told that we would subsequently fail our exams and not be able to graduate. My father did not take this lying down, he went to the superintendent of Greenville City schools, Mr. C.C. Cleetwood, and we were allowed to come back to school after the others had gone home, and take our exams. We were also able to graduate with our class on June 1, 1972. I also passed the test to go into the Army on the Buddy/Buddy plan with my friend Edgar Savage. I did this to please my parents, just in case I did not graduate. I did not want to let my parents down and I wanted them to be proud of me for still trying to make something of my life. I placed my baseball dreams on hold and entered the Army on June 16, 1972 and got out on June 16, 1975, with an honorable discharge. I was a member of the 82nd Airborne Division, at Ft. Bragg, NC. My job in the army was a personnel clerk for 18 months with the 82nd ADMIN Co., and I was also a motor pool dispatcher for the 763 Ordinance Company at Fort Bragg, for my last 18 months. While in the army, I had the burning desire to get out and go to college to pursue my dream of playing professional baseball one day. After my discharge, I contacted Coach Russ Frazier at Louisburg Jr. College in November, 1975 about obtaining the opportunity to try out for his team. He told me that his team was already set and he had no more room for another player, other than on the practice squad. So I said, "O.K. I'll take that."

Chapter 3

MY COLLEGE DAYS

I enrolled at Louisburg College in January, 1976 with the hopes of not only making their team, but catching the eyes of the professional baseball scouts that attended their practices and games. I thank God that I had a praying mother, who prayed that God's Favor would be with me. I did make the team in the spring of 1976, and ended up starting in left field. I batted about .315, with about 8 homeruns, and about 15 stolen bases in the spring season. But at that time Louisburg College was playing in a summer league with 4 year schools, such as UNC–Chapel Hill, UNC Wilmington, Elon College, Methodist College, East Carolina Univ., and Atlantic Christian College, which is Barton College of Wilson, NC, today. We finished number one in the Summer League of 1976, I finished with the highest batting average, .369, and most home runs, 11. This is what caught the eyes of the professional baseball scouts because I was playing against a higher caliber of players, and I finished as the most outstanding player of the summer league, and won a scholarship from Louisburg College for my final year.

In April of 1976, my first child was born on the 15th of that month, the late Prophet D. Doc Taylor. Then in January of 1977, the Los Angeles Dodgers selected me in the second round of the Amateur Major League Baseball Draft. I was truly blessed to go from a walk-on, to being a second round draft pick, Praise God! That spring season I helped lead Louisburg College to the Junior College World Series in Grand Junction, Colorado. We did not do well in the World Series because our pitching failed us. We played 2 games and were eliminated because we lost both games. I was blessed to have my parents to fly out to Colorado and see me play in the World Series. I did hit a home run for my parents, and ended up with 3 hits out of 7 at bats, which equals to about a .429 batting average in the World Series. Also on March 1, 1977, I had a son born, Jermaine Carlton Jones. Then on May

18, 1977, I got married to my oldest son's mother, who happened to be pregnant with my daughter, Tameka Lashelle Daniels, who is Mrs. Tameka L. Jones today. So in other words… I had a shot–gun wedding!

Chapter 4

MY PROFESSIONAL BASEBALL DAYS

I left to sign with the Los Angeles Dodgers Rookie League team in Lethbridge Alberta, Canada, in June of 1977. Playing in Canada for the Dodgers Rookie League Team was a great experience. I had some good times and a few bad times there. Lethbridge was a city of about 50,000 people, and only about 75 were black. The people of Lethbridge treated the black ball players with dignity and respect, but I cannot say the same for our fellow teammates and coaches. There were 5 black players on the team, and we felt the racial tension and prejudices coming from our teammates and coaches. We ended up winning the pioneer League Championship, and received Championship rings, the summer of 1977. I had one terrible incident with my head coach, of whom I will only use his initials, G. H., and I was not saved at the time. I was already fed up with the way he was playing me, only using me mostly as a designated hitter, and I knew this was not helping me to get promoted to a higher level, because the teams wanted you to be able to play defense in the field too. My coach was showing favoritism to this other second–baseman, who happened to be white. It was also his second year in Rookie ball, and his dad was a coach with one of the Dodgers other minor league teams. That is when I found out about politics in professional sports.

Anyway, this particular night, I had hit a double, and I ended up scoring from second base, and I had to slide in home plate. When I got back to the dugout, I had pulled down my pants to get the dirt out of the inside of my pants, and pull my socks back up, because I always liked to look neat in my uniform. So my coach made the remark, "I would not expose those legs if I was you." That's when I went off on him, and cursed him, and called him a redneck M.F. This was way out of character for me, because I was raised better than that, but I had taken all I could take from him. Even though I apologized the next day, he held a grudge against me for a whole year. I learned that you cannot lash out at people who hold your future in their hands. This is the first time I had to deal with rejection like that, especially coming from a coach. All of my coaches before liked me a lot, white and black, up until this point in my career. I realized then that I do not handle rejection well. It also taught me that none of us know everything about anything, and we must remain humble and teachable throughout life. We must realize that it's a time to speak up for yourself, the right way, and a time to keep your mouth shut, especially when it is gonna offend others who can help you or hurt you, when it comes to evaluating your attitude and performance.

I ended up finishing the season without another incident, but the damage was done as far as he was concerned. I finished that year with a .299 batting average, with 6 home runs, and 18 stolen bases and about 45 RBI's. The following year 1978, I was invited to the Dodgers spring training camp in Vero Beach, Florida. I left for spring training in March of 1978. While on the way, my plane stopped at the airport in Atlanta, Georgia, in order for me to change to catch a flight to Vero Beach, FL I used the restroom at the airport, and took off my Rookie League Championship ring to wash my hands, and got caught up in a conversation with a gentleman about spring training and forgot my ring. I headed back to the restroom and discovered that my ring was gone. Boy was I hurt. It was a very nice ring, similar to a high school class ring, but much prettier with a diamond in the center of it. It was engraved with the name of the team, the year, and on the inside of it, my name and number. I realized then that I was starting spring training off on a wrong note. After getting to camp, I had a chance to mingle with the Dodgers big league players, such as Steve Garvey, Dusty Baker, Reggie Smith, Steve Yeager, Davey Lopes, Ron Cey, and Mike Scioscia, and Manager Tommy Lasorda.

I had a chance to shake hands with Don Newcombe, who was a hall of fame Dodgers pitcher, and Roy Campanella, who was a hall of fame catcher for the Dodgers. I also had a chance to see Reggie Jackson for the first time in person. I was in spring

Rise Again

training for more than a week, when I got an emergency phone call about my oldest sister, Josette Daniels, being in an automobile accident. I did not know how serious she had been hurt. Immediately I asked for permission to fly home to see about my sister, it was granted. I was told to try to make it back in 3 days if I could. After getting to the hospital and seeing her, I began to cry, because she was swollen so badly, she was almost unrecognizable, and the doctors were talking in circles about her condition. Anyway, I returned to spring training a week later, thinking that everything was o.k. Three days after getting back, I was released by the Dodgers, because they felt I had missed too much practice, plus the fact that I had a snobby attitude with the Dodgers management because they felt like my sister's accident was not that serious for me to be gone a whole week. One of the coaches that helped make that decision about releasing me was my Rookie League coach, G.H. He already had it in for me from the incident the year before. I must admit it took me by surprise, because I knew I was one of the best players in camp. A lot of those guys could not carry my bags, if you know what I mean. But when it was all said and done, it was my mouth and arrogant attitude that cost me a chance of making the Dodgers big league team. That is also when I remembered those words I read a while back, "Your Attitude determines your Altitude in life".

Chapter 5

COMING BACK HOME

My son Terrell was born on April 30, 1978. So after coming back home to Greenville, NC, I got a call about an independent team in Alexandria, Va., that was having a tryout. I went up for the tryout, got signed by them to contract, but I was upset about what happened with the Dodgers. I was not happy because I was not where I wanted to be, and my playing really showed it. I felt like a reject. I did finish the year in Alexandria, Va., playing with the Alexandria Dukes.

The following year I was contacted by a scout for the Pittsburgh Pirates, named Murray Cooke, and he invited me to a tryout in Salem, Va. He was very impressed with my speed, my hitting with power for a small man, and my range at second base. So he signed me to another contract to play for their minor league team in Shelby, NC. I felt good about myself again, because I was playing for the Pittsburgh Pirates, an organization that really believed in giving Blacks and other minorities a fair chance to make it to the big leagues. I had a good year with the Shelby team, I batted about .305, with about 9 home runs, and 22 stolen bases, and about 68 RBI's. I saved several games with spectacular plays at second base. They told me that in order for me to get to the big leagues I would need to have surgery on my right elbow to be able to get more velocity on my throwing. They explained that I could be able to turn the double play at second base a lot quicker, because the guys in the big leagues were a lot faster than most of the guys in the minor leagues. The reason they suggested this was because I injured my elbow when I was in the army, and had surgery, which caused my throwing to lose some velocity. So I agreed to have surgery in December of 1979, at Pitt Memorial Hospital in Greenville, NC, by a specialist named Dr. Bowman. All went well with the surgery. I was invited to the Pittsburgh Pirates spring training camp in Bradenton, FL in March of 1980. I was excited because the

Rise Again

Pirates had just won the World Series in October of 1979. I got a chance to eat, sleep, and practice with the World Series Champions, how blessed I was. I got a chance to shake hands and talk to guys like Big Dave Parker, Willie "POPS" Stargell, Omar Moreno, Manny Sanguillen, Phil Garner, Tim Foli, John Candelaria, and the manager of the team, Chuck Tanner. These guys were normal down to earth guys. Not long after being in spring training, my joy and excitement turned to disappointment. My elbow was paining me a lot whenever I would throw. Then it began to swell and not go down. The trainers for the Pirates, looked at it, examined it, and could not understand why it was swelling so much, because the ex-rays showed it was healing from the surgery. I was not saved then, so I did not pray and ask God to heal it. This went on for about 2 weeks. The management for the Pirates told me that they was sorry, but they had to release me, because my elbow may never get back to where I could throw with good velocity, and be pain free. They told me they hated it from me, because I was a helluva ball player, but I had a handicap, and this was a business, and they had to move on in another direction. Those words really crushed my spirit. But in June of 1980, I felt joy again because that is when my son, Donnie was born on June 4, 1980.

Chapter 6

LIFE AFTER BASEBALL

After returning home from the Pirates Spring Training camp, I had a reality check, and I asked myself, where do I go from here? By this time I had a wife and 5 children, and I knew I had to get a real job now, because it seemed that my baseball career was over. I got a job working on a trash truck for the city of Greenville, NC. This job was pretty easy, just going around picking up front yard household goods, like old couches, refrigerators that were worn out, clothes that were no good anymore, and T.V's that were broken. I did this for about 8 months, and then I started having a pity party, feeling sorry for myself, thinking about what had happened to my baseball career. One day, I was heading to the major leagues in baseball, and then all of a sudden, I was back home working on the trash truck, for about $5.00 an hour. I began to develop a "don't care" attitude about life in general. I became bitter towards people. Instead of me putting my family first, and doing all I could do to make them happy, I began to neglect them. I did not realize at the time, that there was more to life than baseball. I could not put it behind me.

One day, my brother told me about a friend of his that could help me make some easy money. So I quit the city of Grenville, because I knew I did not belong there anyway. My brother's friend, Mr. Bigg, began to front me pounds of marijuana in the spring of 1981. By this time I was smoking marijuana and drinking beer, trying to ease the pain of my broken dreams. I got involved in an extra marital affair. This woman treated me like a king, and did for my kids too, like she was their mother, especially at Christmas time and on their birthdays. I did pretty good, money-wise, with the marijuana, and then I started selling cocaine too, for this same man. Not long after selling cocaine, I stopped selling the marijuana, and moved up to selling heroin, along with the cocaine, because these two went together anyway.

Rise Again

Most of my cocaine users were heroin users also, so I began to realize that I could make a lot more money selling both of them. I did not realize at the time, it also brought on a lot more heat from law enforcement too. I was able to do pretty good with these 2 products, because I was not using them myself at the time. After about 2 years of selling heroin and cocaine, out of curiosity, in 1983, I decided to try snorting both of them, because they do come in powder form. I was too afraid of needles, so I knew shooting it into my veins was out of the question. I only decided to try them after hearing all the talk about how it makes you feel, and how you are able to satisfy more than one woman in the same day, so my curiosity got the best of me, I just had to see for myself if what I had heard was true. I found out it was true, but I also found something else, that when you use heroin for 3 straight days, you have become addicted to it. I eventually became my best customer. To be honest with you, I liked the way that heroin made me feel. It had me thinking I was the most intelligent guy, it made me happy, very playful, and I could not get enough sex. Then too, it helped me to escape the pain of my baseball dream being crushed. It gave me a false sense of security, and I finally realized I was only trying to escape reality. My habit brought on strife and friction in my marriage, with my wife, kids, and other family members, especially my brother, Jeffrey. He was always coming to my rescue whenever my money was short on my heroin package, so that the man that was fronting us the dope, would not retaliate with violence when he did not get all of his money. This man Mr. Bigg, was known to hurt you, if you came up short more than twice. It got to the point that I came up short almost every week, because I knew that my brother would bail me out. One day my brother, just told me, "J.C., you are not gonna keep using me like that to bail you out every week, it don't make sense." It caused us to start drifting away from each other. This hurt a lot because Jeff was my best friend, too, but I continued to do things that would piss my brother off, like getting packages from other drug dealers and not paying them. My brother would hear about it, and try to talk to the dealers, and work something out with them to get them paid. I did not realize what a monster of a habit I had. I began to even take food from my family, by selling the food stamps that

Rise Again

social services had given me, to get my drugs. I was not working at the time, and I was able to get about $350.00 a month in food stamps, of which only about $100.00, if that, went into food for my family. This went on for about 16 months, and then one day, I got somewhat of a wake-up call. The Greenville Police came with a warrant for my arrest for selling 150 bags of heroin; and a half- ounce of cocaine to the undercover SBI agent. They also had a warrant for my brother, Jeffrey, for conspiracy to sell heroin and cocaine, because he had given me a ride to 2 of the transactions with the SBI agent. This was February of 1984. My brother and I were put under a $20,000 cash bond. My brother got the man, Mr. Bigg, to put up his bond, because they were still on good terms, plus my brother had made this man plenty of money. I was the one left in jail, broke, busted, and disgusted, looking stupid. But I worried my dear mother every day for 4 days, morning, noon, and night to get me out. She in turn worried my father, because my father had refused to get me out, because he reminded me of what I had told him when he tried to get me to stop selling drugs and using drugs. I told him; that I was grown, I no longer stayed under his roof, and I'm big enough to deal with the consequences, if I did get busted. I don't know what my mother said to him, but after letting me sit there for 4 days and nights, he finally came and got me out of jail. When I walked out of jail that night I ran up to my father and kissed him on the jaw. I was just that happy to see him. That was my first time spending the night in jail, and I did not like being there. My brother and I went back to court July 16, 1984. We were facing 10 to 20 years, in prison, even though it was our first offense. There were 3 transactions with the SBI agent, who was posing as a pimp, with 2 prostitutes, when he came to us. I sold him 50 bags of heroin, 2 times, and the third transaction; I sold him 50 bags of heroin and a half ounce of cocaine. There would of have been a fourth transaction with him, but I took the $600, in brand new 20 dollars bills and ran. So when we came to court on the 16th of July, 1984, I pleaded guilty to all of the charges, and I did my best to free my brother. I told the judge that the drugs were mine, and my brother only gave me a ride, not knowing what I was doing when I went to meet these people. So that saved my brother, 2 years in prison, but he still got 2 years for conspiracy, because they had him on tape on one of the transactions, talking to me about the money for the drugs. So instead of getting four years in prison, he got 2 years, and he ended up doing 11 months of the 2 year sentence. The judge was supposed to have given me the maximum sentence that he could, but he didn't, because I had a few mitigating factors in my favor: 1. I was a heroin addict, that went to rehab for 27 days, 2. my parents were outstanding citizens in the community, 3. I was a veteran of the US Army, with a honorable discharge, 4. I was an ex-professional baseball player, and 5. It was my first offense. So instead of a 10 to 20 year sentence, I ended up with a 6 year sentence, with immediate work release. My mother broke down in tears that day, because both of her sons were going to prison. I will never forget her words to us, she said, "I love you, and Jesus loves you, and He still has a plan and purpose for your lives." She told us to stay strong, and keep our heads up, and pray, because Jesus is still the answer to all of your problems. I did not know when I left that courtroom that day that I still had some pending charges from some other drug sales I had made.

My brother and I were in the Pitt County Jail, in Greenville, NC for about 30 days, and then we were transferred off to be processed at Wayne Correctional Center, in Goldsboro, NC. We were there for about 2 months, and my brother was transferred to an honor grade camp, in Maury, NC. Since I had more than 2 years, I was transferred to a medium security camp, or gun camp, at Creswell, NC. It was known as Sutton plantation, because the superintendent there was Mr. Sutton, and he was tough. I did not know it at the time, but he was a friend of my father's. On January 31, 1985, they took me back to court in Greenville, NC to answer those pending charges. I pleaded guilty again, and I was blessed because the judge could have given me a 3 year sentence to run consecutive with the current sentence that I had. That meant I would have had to do it after finishing my 6 year sentence. But because I had a praying mother, and the favor of God, which I did not understand at that time, was with me, I received a 3 year sentence to run concurrently with my present sentence that I was doing. That meant I did not have to do any extra time after the 6 year sentence was up. My mother was present again in the courtroom that day, and she came up to me and gave me a kiss, told me she loved me, Jesus loves me, and that when all else fails, continue to trust Jesus! When my mother left the courtroom that day, a strange feeling came over me, and I broke down in tears. I saw the pain and hurt in her eyes, from what my brother and I had put her through. In fact, I am breaking down in tears right now; because it was the last time my mother laid eyes on me and spoke to me. She was diagnosed with a tumor in her stomach in March, 1985 by Dr. Andrew Best. She told him she did not want him to operate on her. She told me in her last letter to me, about March 22, 1985 that she was trusting God to heal her, and she said that she was standing on God's Word, in 1st Peter 2:24, by Jesus she was healed. If that was His will for her at that time, or else she was going home to be with the Lord. She also told me, in that last letter that God had promised to save her whole household, whether she was alive to see it, or not, she knew it would come to pass, HALLELUJAH!!!

I received an emergency phone call from home on April 10, 1985 telling me that the doctor had said that my mother only had a few days to live. So on April 11, 1985 the camp superintendent, Mr. Sutton, arranged for me to be taken home to visit my mother at Pitt Memorial Hospital, in Greenville, NC. I was supposed to have been taken in shackles and leg irons for my 2 hour visit with my mother, but the guards that took me, had compassion on me, and took off the shackles and leg irons, and let me visit with my mother, one on one. PRAISE GOD!!!! She was in and out of consciousness, but she could not speak, because of the pain shots she was given. She still recognized who I was, because I would ask her certain things and she would squeeze my hand to let me know that she heard me. Even though the visit was for 2 hours, it seemed like a very short time.

On the way back to the camp, I thought I would break down and cry, but I didn't. Instead, I was calm and a peace came over me, assuring me that my mother was looking forward to going home to be with the Lord! She knew what the Bible said in 2nd Corinthians: 5-6 "to be absent from the body, is to be present with the Lord". Then on April 15, 1985 early that morning, I got

Rise Again

the news that my mother had gone home to be with the Lord. This was my oldest son's ninth birthday, the late Prophet D. Doc Taylor, the grandson who loved to go to church with his grandmother. He was also the one that God had shown my mother in a dream, when he was 7 years old, that he would be in the pulpit preaching the gospel of Jesus Christ, and it came to pass on Feb. 25, 1996. How befitting for God to take my mother home to be with Him on his birthday. It seemed like my whole world came crashing down that day. My mind became very foggy from that day, until about 3 months after her death. I questioned God as to why He would take my mother at such a young age; 49 years old. Especially since, she was busy preaching the Gospel, going to the nursing homes, prison camps, and hospitals, telling people about the love of Jesus Christ. A minister friend of mine told me that being with Jesus is far greater for your mother, than her being on earth with her husband and children. He said death is but a gain of Glory, for those that are in Jesus Christ. He quoted Psalm 116:15, "Precious in the sight of the Lord is the death of His saints." Then he gave me something to think about, he said, "Would you have wanted your mother to be healed temporarily, because God could have done that, by taking the cancer from her, or would you want her to be healed permanently, by God taking her from the cancer, from the pain and hurts of this cruel world, where she won't have to suffer no more?" Then, I realized I was only being selfish, because I wanted her to stay here for us. I also thought to myself, who am I to question God, He knows what's best for all of us. I began to remember the words that my mother used to tell us, "When I lay my head down for good, you will see the world in a lot of different light." She would tell us, you got to get it right with God because you must give an account for yourselves of the deeds done in your body. It then began to sink in that I have to seek God for myself. Because as long as my mother was living, I felt like I was alright, I did not have to pray for myself, because my mother was always praying for us. It was like she was our crutch that we could lean on, instead of God. Whenever we had problems in life, we could always go to her, and it seemed like we always got an answer or solution to the problem. Now I can relate to what Isaiah was saying in Isaiah 6:1 in the

Rise Again

year that King Uzziah died, I saw the Lord sitting on a throne, high and lifted up, and the train of His robe filled the temple. Sometimes God has to remove people out of lives, so that we esteem higher in Him, and that we can see Him clearer! I became somewhat distant after my mother's death and burial, I mean distant from people that I was incarcerated with. Once I made work release, I would begin to open up again to a degree. The devil tried to put that thought in my mind that my brother and I caused our mother to go to an early grave. By me not being saved, I did not have anything to fight off those thoughts. I began to get home passes during the week, wherein; my best friend from my childhood, Larry Dixon, would sponsor me out twice a week on 6 hour passes. Every other weekend my first wife would come and sign me out for 48 hour home passes. So this helped me to come around a lot too. I eventually finished my first prison stint, on July 22, 1986, after doing 2 yrs., and 5 days on a 6 year sentence. From the time I got out, I drifted around going from job to job and eventually moved to Portsmouth VA with my first wife to see if a change of scenery would help out marriage. We were slowly drifting apart. We tried this for 4 years.

Chapter 7

MY FIRST RELEASE

My wife and kids welcomed me home with open arms, hoping that I had changed. But I quickly realized that I had not. After being home for about a month, I eventually got right back into hustling, because I could not find a job. I also returned to using drugs again. So after putting up with this for about a year, my wife told me that she was tired of living like that and she wanted to move back home to Portsmouth, Va., to be near her mother, and the rest of her family. In October of 1987, she made good on her threat. She packed up her things, and my 4 children, and moved back to Portsmouth, Va. I was given an ultimatum, if I wanted to be with her and my kids, I had to leave Greenville, N.C., and be drug-free. So after about 3 weeks of missing them, I sold the rest of my furniture, and moved to Portsmouth, Va. At first her parents, seemed to not want me there. So after I convinced them that I really wanted to work things out and be with my family, they finally agreed to me being there. I asked them to give me about a month to find a place for my family, and we would be out of their house. So I got a job as a laborer for a brick mason company, and she was already working at McDonald's. My father-in-law charged me $75.00 a week rent, and we had to buy our own groceries. It took us about 6 weeks to save up about $850.00, enough for a deposit, and first month rent. We found a lovely 3 bedroom apartment in the Cherokee Park section of Portsmouth. I had stopped doing drugs, and was really trying to make my marriage work. I was working, I had bought a car from my father, I got my 3 boys involved in the Little League baseball team, and I was attending PTA meetings at their school, so life seemed to be back on the right track. I was clean for about 2 years, and then I got the urge to get high again. I started this time snorting a little cocaine, and then that heroin spirit rose up in me again. I did not realize at the time that those spirits are just lying dormant in you, and unless God delivers you of them, they will keep returning to you. That is when I found out that Portsmouth was called the heroin capital of the East Coast. It is so plentiful there and cheap, compared to what it cost in Greenville. It was $10 a cap, and it was $20 a bag in Greenville, and the quantity was the same. Now that I was no longer hustling to support my habit, I began to be late with my rent and light bill, and before long I was facing evictions and cut off notices, in fact my lights were cut off twice behind my drug habit. I found myself hanging out in some of the most notorious projects in the world, Ida Barbour, Lincoln Park, and Jeffrey Wilson housing projects, because this is where you found the good heroin. Then sometimes we would ride to the projects in Norfolk, which was right through the Portsmouth Tunnel, to Calvary Park, Young's Park, and Robert's park housing projects. These projects were dangerous at 12:00 noon, but when you got a drug habit, you don't care; you just gotta take a chance to get your dope. I was running and ripping through these places all times of day and night. When you are strung out on heroin, it causes you to be on the prowl early in the morning until late at night. You are either looking for the drugs, or either planning schemes of where your next lick is gonna be, to get your money for your next fix. This brought on a lot of arguments and controversy in my marriage again. My wife threatened to leave me again. One day, I was working with a friend of mine named Lindsey Brinkley, and we were doing some electrical work for a Pastor named C.V. Russell, Jr. I began to talk to this preacher about his church, and he was telling me about the wonderful things that God was doing in his church. This caught my attention, plus the way that this man came out there where we were working and getting his hands dirty too helping us, along with having his wife feed us. This got me curious enough to want to go and check out his church. In March of 1990, I did go to his church on Church St., Mt. Carmel Baptist Church. I was impressed right away when I got there; because of the love they showed you when they greeted you. Then the service itself was wonderful, it was like being in a nightclub, but only you were jamming for the Lord. I knew right away this was not your average Baptist church. Then in the middle of the service right before the word came forth, the Pastor's daughter, Missy Russell, she was 10 years old at the time, sang a song that has

Rise Again

been on my heart and in my spirit ever since. She sang the song, I Love You, I Love You, I Love You Lord today because you cared for me in such a special way. That's why I praise you, I lift you up, and I magnify your name. That's why my heart is filled with praise, my heart, my mind, my soul belongs to you. You paid the price for me way back on Calvary. That's why I praise you, I lift you up, and I magnify your name, that's why my heart is filled with praise. She repeated it 2 times. Before I knew it I was shedding tears, because I did want to change my life, and I knew that God was the answer, and after the word came forth, it brought about more conviction, so when altar call came, I ran down to the altar, because I was tired of living like I was living, and continuing to hurt my family because of my drug addiction. I asked Jesus to come into my heart and be my Lord and Savior, Alleluia! I returned back home that day and told my wife what I had done, and she said, yeah right, in a very sarcastic way. This pissed me off at first, because I was serious about what I had just done. Anyway I was going to church every Sunday, and I even stopped using drugs again for about 6 months. My children even joined me at Mt. Carmel.

Chapter 8

IT'S OVER

In December of 1990, I caught my wife at another man's house, when she was supposed to have been at work. This was the same man that I had seen drop her off at home, supposedly after she had gotten off work. I asked her what was really going on and she broke down and told me, so I asked her to come and get her clothes and leave, and I would take care of my kids. So she did for about 2 weeks, and then my kids begged me to let their mother come home to be with them for Christmas, and I did. She ended up staying until that March of 1991, and we separated for good. She had gotten her a 3 bedroom house in Portsmouth, and I allowed her to take the kids, because I knew they wanted to be with their mother. I rented a room from Mrs. Sonia Roundtree, a beautiful Christian woman, in Norfolk, Va., who owned a rooming house. This woman began to pray for me and my family, and encouraged me to turn things over to Jesus, and let Him work things out. She reminded me so much of my mother. I was going to church all the time, not just on Sundays. I was working with a janitorial service at the time too. I got me another car and I would go and get my kids on Sundays to go to church, and sometimes I would keep my boys for the weekend. I would still go to their schools for parent teacher's conferences, and I would still attend my boys' baseball games. I also remained celibate the first 2 years of my separation, and I was drug-free. I wanted God to fix my marriage, because I liked family life, and I was missing being there with my children. Then I began to realize that I had driven my wife into the arms of another man. My drug addiction and my infidelity drove her to do what she did. You see, I know at one time, she really loved me and did all she could to make it work. But after 14 ½ years, she had taken all she could handle. After 2 years of praying and hoping that we could get back together, I was ready to move on with my life, because I saw that she was happy and was not coming back. That's when I began to search for another wife. I

Rise Again

began dating a woman in my church from Brooklyn, NY. We both backslid because we started having sex, and we were not married. She had just divorced a year earlier, and I had not healed from my separation from my wife. That is when I first learned that hurt people, hurt people. My relationship with this lady lasted about 9 months. I had stopped going to church because I was feeling guilty that just about everyone in the church knew we were sleeping together, and I felt like a hypocrite. In February of 1994, I began another relationship with another young lady named Janet. She was an independent woman, with her own apartment, her own car, plus she was the manager of this taco restaurant. Even though I knew I was out of the will of God, I was still trying to find love and happiness, and make these relationships work. By this time I was working at the Portsmouth Naval Shipyard as a painter, making $12.50 an hour. I also had my own apartment and a car, and it seemed as if I was finally getting somewhere in life. In other words, I thought I had it going on again. Then in October of 1994, I got word that my Father did not have long to live, he was suffering with colon cancer. This was a terrible blow to me, because my father, was always the backbone of our family, and I had never seen him sick a day in my life. I just had a feeling that somehow he would overcome the cancer. When I went home to see him that October, I just broke down and cried, because my father looked like a skeleton, that's how much damage the cancer had done to his body. When he was healthy, he was a very handsome man, 6 feet 2 inches tall, and 250 pounds of nothing but muscle. He was about 95 pounds, when I saw him in this state. But the good news is he was saved and baptized, Alleluia!! That gave me some consolation, but it still did not ease the pain in my heart, because reality began to set in, that I really was gonna lose my father. I did not know I truly cared that much for him, until I began to think that he would not be in my life anymore. You see, my father was a very strict disciplinarian, and my siblings and I used to think he was so mean. But I truly appreciate having a father like the late Mr. Jessie Lee Daniels, Jr., I am thankful today for all that he taught me about life and those things that he instilled in me. My daddy was a man's man, because he was always respected and admired by other men. Even though he had his flows, he was the best father and provider any child would want, other than Jesus Christ. On Feb.13, 1995 my father went home to be with the Lord. In a way, I was glad to see him out of his pain and suffering. My father was a good man according to Prov. 13:22 because he left an inheritance for his children and grandchildren, but especially his grandchildren. When his will was read by his attorney, it shocked us all, because we did not know that he had left that much to us. He was a self-made millionaire, when you add up his money and property. You could never tell whether he was a poor man or rich man, because he was the same all the time. But he believed in helping others. He was never a flashy dresser, or driving a Mercedes or Cadillac, in other words, a show off. One of his favorite sayings was, "It is better to have a million dollars, than try to look like a million dollars".

Chapter 9

SAYING GOODBYE

After my father's death, I began to think who is gonna be next in my family to die. So it also made me think about my life, and where was it headed. I wanted to change, but I was too weak in my flesh to do it. I eventually started going back to church, but that did not last too long, because I got tired of being convicted by the word of God, every time I would go. The devil was feeding my mind with all kinds of crazy thoughts, making me think, you're all right, you got plenty of time to get it right. My relationship with Janet began to get rocky, we started arguing at each other, it seemed like every other day. Then, before you know it, I was back snorting heroin again, to escape the reality of what was going on in my life. This really pissed Janet off because I had told her I would not mess with that stuff again. I had been clean about 2 ½ years. Things got so bad that I ended up spending most of my money that my father had left me, on heroin, and I eventually lost my apartment. Janet allowed me to move in with her. I can now elate to the prodigal son in Luke 15:11-31, he squandered his inheritance on riotous living. In April of 1996, I got busted with about $90.00 worth of cocaine that I was on my way to trade off for some heroin. This happened while walking through a mostly white middle class neighborhood of Norfolk, Va., the Sherwood Forest section, in the middle of the day. I was only about 4 blocks from where I stayed, and 2 undercover officers in a plain car approached me and asked me for my I.D. I panicked and ran when I realized they were police, because I knew I had the crack cocaine on me, and I wanted to get away far enough from them to get the crack off of me. I ran about 5 ½ blocks, then I ditched the crack, which was in a Ziploc freezer bag, under a city of Norfolk maintenance truck. When I had gotten it off of me, police cars came from everywhere. So I just calmly slowed down and walked up to them, because they had me surrounded by this time. They asked me why did I run, and I told them I was afraid, because I did not

Rise Again

know who the 2 undercover officers were, I did not know if they intended to rob me or what. Then they asked me did I know who had been breaking into those homes in that neighborhood and, I told them, I did not know, but it was not me, and at this time I was telling them the truth. So they ran a background check on me, and it came back clean, and they were just about to let me go, when another police car pulled up alongside of the car I was sitting in, dangling the Ziploc bag with the crack cocaine in it. One of those city workers saw me when I threw the bag under the truck, and being a good law abiding citizen, he flagged the police down, gave it to him, and told him that the guy you all were chasing just threw it under the truck. I denied it all the way to the police station, until they wiped the bag for fingerprints. They arrested me and put me under a $2500.00 bond. I called Janet, and she refused to come and get me, and told me this is what I needed. I stayed in jail about 5 days, and then my check from my job at the shipyard came. Janet cashed it for me, and gave the money to my friend, Ike, who I worked with. He got in touch with a bondsman, who got me out. It was out about 2 months before I took a plea bargain for one year, and one year probation, plus community service. I ended up doing 9 months and 3 days on that sentence.

Chapter 10

JANET TAKES ME BACK

I pleaded with Janet to take me back in, and I would get my life back on track, and she felt sorry for me again and took me back in, this was May of 1997. She told me these words one day, and I never forgot them, "Jessie, if you ever get off of those drugs, you will make somebody a good husband, and I believe you will become that man of God, that you desire to be." She told me, "That is why the devil is trying to keep you bound, because he knows you are a threat to him. I can see God using you one day, when you overcome this weakness." Those words never were far from my memory, because they helped me to be determined to beat that habit. Just to know that at least one person still believed in me, gave me hope. I am forever grateful to her for having told me what she saw in me, because it helped me not to totally give up. She knew I wanted to serve God in some capacity, because every time I would be high on heroin, I would start quoting scriptures, and actually preach a short sermon. That was where my heart was, on being an awesome man of God. My mind was willing, but my flesh was weak. Janet and I went through 2 more years of a rocky relationship. It seemed like every other week we would get into arguments, because I was still slipping and using heroin, and she could tell, and I would act like I was upset and leave, that is when she did not put me out. I would go and find an abandoned house and stay there for about 3 or 4 more days, until I couldn't take it anymore, then come up with some more money, and go and buy Janet something nice and she would let me back into her home. During this time, I was supporting my habit by any means necessary, and I literally mean that, except I did not take a gun and rob anyone, but I stole in other ways to support my habit. I had lost my job at the shipyard when I went to prison those 9 months. By this time, hustling on the street was easier than trying to find a job. Janet put up with me until about October of 1999, and that is when we really said our final good-byes, because she had taken all she could take. It hurt me because I had messed up a good thing. She was a woman that wanted things in life, and she was full of ambition. In fact, as I write this book, she is the owner of that taco restaurant that she used to manage while we were involved. I roamed the streets of Norfolk, Va. another 2 years, doing the same things, getting high, staying in abandoned houses, eating in soup kitchens in order to survive.

Chapter 11

MY SECOND MARRIAGE

I still had the desire to have another wife, so I decided to give my college sweetheart a call. She also happened to be my second oldest son's mother, Lois Jean Jones, of Louisburg, NC. We began talking and eventually dating again. The Lord blessed me to stop using drugs a while, and I led her to the Lord. We got married on May 4, 2001. I was not able to move right away to Louisburg, because of my probation requirements in Norfolk. But I did move to Louisburg, NC in July of 2002. I felt good about the move, because it made me feel refreshed, after the 15 tumultuous years in Portsmouth and Norfolk, Va. I thought when I left Louisburg College in 1977, that I would only go back to visit my son, Jermaine Jones. That place was way out in the sticks to me, and I could not imagine myself actually settling down and living there. I was used to living in much larger cities, with much more to do. The opportunities there were slim to none. But actually that was the place I needed to be, to help me slow down on my riotous living, and get back on track with God. I got a job doing landscaping work, my wife and I joined Abundant Life Christian Center, off Old Poole Rd. in Raleigh, NC. We were introduced to this church, by our late son, Prophet D. "Doc" Taylor. We really enjoyed being there. In October of 2002, I found myself back on heroin. I would make trips to Greenville, N.C, my hometown, back and forth to Portsmouth, VA and then to Durham, NC to buy heroin. It got to the point, where I would write checks on my wife's checking account. I began taking money out of her pocketbook late nights after she had fallen asleep. Then it got so bad that I started indulging in stolen goods, especially lawn equipment. I began to cry out to God, because I was getting sick and tired of living like I was living. My wife threatened to separate from me if I did not change, because she did not want to be with a drug addict the rest of her life. The bad part about this was that I was still going to church at Abundant Life Christian Center every Sunday. I could not figure out, why I could stop doing heroin for a while only to return to it. Then on November 18, 2003, the Durham County Sheriffs stopped me in Durham, after I was seen coming out of a man's shed in his backyard with 2 weed-eaters. I was headed to sale them for more heroin. What I don't understand is, I had already done 2 bags of heroin about 8 am that morning, and I had 2 more bags on me, which I quickly stashed in a secret place in my Kia truck, and $300 home in my suit coat pocket. So I really did not need to steal anything at that time. Anyway, I called my wife to tell her what happened, because they impounded her Kia truck, and that really pissed her off. That was our only transportation at that time. So she had to pay someone to pick her up from work and take her to get her truck from the place where it was towed to. When she got there, the man that towed the vehicle, told my wife that several people were out trying to locate the driver of a green Kia, who had been terrorizing their community with late night break-ins into their lawn sheds. They wanted to do some serious harm to whoever it was. They told her she had better get out of Durham quick, before someone thought she had something to do with it. Anyway, I stayed in jail that night, since I had to go before the judge the next morning. I was put under a $1000 bond. My wife came up the next day to pay a bondsman to get me out. She used my $300 that I had stashed away in my suit pocket to get me out. We argued all the way from Durham to Louisburg, which is 45 miles apart, and then some. Then on November 23, 2003 the Franklin County Sheriff's officers and detectives stopped me, and questioned me about some lawn equipment, and they had me red-handed with surveillance pictures and license tags. They questioned me about some other incidents so I just took them to the places where I had hit. By this time, I was so tired of the direction my life was going in, I just felt like this was God's way of slowing me down before I got killed out there in my mess. I knew I was gonna be there until I got sentenced for these charges. This is no lie, it seemed like a 100 lbs. weight was lifted off of me.

Chapter 12

MY LAST TIME IN PRISON

Not long after being in Franklin County jail, I fell on my knees, and I cried out to God, "Please help me not to go back to this lifestyle that was destroying me." I repented of my wrong-doings, and I thanked God for not allowing me to die out there in my mess.

I knew He had forgiven me, because in 1 John 1:9, it says, if we confess our sins, He is faithful and just to forgive us our sins and to cleanse us of all unrighteousness. Then I read in Jeremiah 3:14, where it says, "Return o backsliding children, says the Lord, for I am married to you".

Once I had gotten back into right standing with God, I began to pray for God to show me what He would have me to do while I was there in Franklin County jail. I began to hold Bible study about 5 times a week; after all there was not much else to do. It gave me a chance to draw closer to God in a way that I never experienced before. My Bible study began to grow from 3 men to about 8 men. The Lord began to answer a lot of prayers for us. Before I went to Superior court for my charges, I asked the Lord to grant me mercy, but let me be able to accept whatever punishment He allowed to come my way. I was sentenced to 30 to 40 months in May of 2004. By the time I left Franklin county jail, over 10 men had gotten saved, and several more had rededicated their lives back to Christ. Also in March of 2004, I had received 12 months and 3 yrs. Probation, for the Durham charges which would run concurrently with my Franklin County sentence. I had asked God to use me for His Glory on every prison camp, he allowed me to go to, because I knew it was better for me to do my time with Jesus, than without him. The first camp I was shipped to was Craven Correctional Facility in Vanceboro, NC. I held Bible study there about 3 times a week. After 3 weeks there, I was shipped to Wayne Correctional Facility for the 45 day DARE program, which is a drug program in Goldsboro, NC. I held Bible study there about 2 times a week, because there were other brothers there that were already holding Bible study, and I would join in with them. There were about 5 men that God saved during my 45 day stay at Wayne Correctional facility from those Bible studies I held there. I had 3 options, to pick from after I had completed the drug program. The only one I prayed for, was Franklin Correctional Facility in Bunn, NC, because my son, Jermaine Jones, was there serving a 30 year sentence for armed robbery, cocaine charges, and assault. He was 17 years old when this occurred back in 1994, and was now 27 years old in 2004. I wanted to be with him, so that we could get to know each other. He was the son that I did not raise, God granted me this, and in September of 2004, I was shipped to Bunn, NC. My intentions was not only to get to know my son, but to show him that his Dad was really a good man, and that I truly loved him, just as much as I did my other 4 children. Plus I was hoping to get him saved.

So after getting to Bunn I began another Bible study in my dorm, because I saw how God had used me at those other camps. That is why I know today, that God can use anyone right where they are at in life, as long as you are willing and available to be used by him. He takes ordinary people to do extraordinary things.

One day, while sitting on my bunk, I asked God why did I keep going back to heroin. He revealed to me that I was trying to stop by my own strength, and I did not totally surrender everything to Him. He took me to Luke 11:24, 25, that says, "When an unclean spirit goes out of man, he goes through dry places, seeking rest, and finding none, he says, I will return to my house from which I came, and when he comes, he finds it swept, and put in order. Then he goes and takes with him seven other spirits, more wicked than himself, and they enter and dwell there, and the last state of that man is worse than the first". I truly know this to be so!

God revealed to me, that my weaknesses and habits were not by accident. God deliberately allowed them in my life for the purpose of demonstrating His power through me, so that He can get the Glory.

Then I told God one day, I want to do more for Him, other than just Bible study. I began to write out scriptures and words of encouragement and inspiration for the inmates and officers there. I would write out about 25 everyday, tell them to pass them on to others. I truly felt the power and Anointing of God on me. I would pray for people and they would be healed, and the officers and inmates started calling me (Preacher-Man). But I earned that nickname, because I was truly walking the walk and talking the talk, and signs and wonders were truly following me, to God Be the Glory!!!!

While in Bunn prison I would occupy my time with praying, reading and studying the word of God, playing basketball, fellowshipping, and worship services on Sunday mornings. We would have Bible study about 3 times a week in the different dorms. In August of 2005, I got a phone call about my brother, Jeffrey Daniels, he had fallen in the parking lot of a restaurant after leaving church that Sunday, and he was in a coma. I immediately went and found a couple of my Christian brothers there, Anthony, Shawn, Terrance and TJ, and we began to touch and agree in prayer that God was gonna bring him out of that coma. Three days later he did come out of the coma. The doctors found a tumor on his brain, and they said it did not look good for him. So I went on a 3 day fast and asked God to heal him and spare his life, and to not allow him to go home to be with him, at least not while I was in prison. God raised my brother up off that hospital bed in August of 2005, and blessed him with 15 more months of life, Praise God. That allowed me to spend 2 ½ months with him, because I got out of prison on September 7, 2006. My brother went home to be with the Lord on November 20, 2006, his oldest son's, Donte Daniels, birthday.

While I was at Bunn prison, the Lord used me to lead at least 25 men to Christ, and another 35 or 40 to rededicate their lives back to Christ, Alleluia! There were about 600 men at Bunn prison while I was there, and I know I had a positive godly impact on at least 200 of those men, to God be the Glory. I am not boasting of myself, just letting others know that God will use you, when you make yourself willing and available to be used by Him. A few of the officers still tell me today that some of the inmates and officers still talk about Brother Jessie Daniels, and that was over 2 years ago when I was last there.

I thank God for all of the awesome men and women of God that came and shared the word of God with us while I was incarcerated, especially the ones that came to Bunn prison, Pastor Lorenzo Peterson, who is my former Bishop, Pastor Mark Hodge and his very loyal and faithful deacons, William Perry, Mike Taylor, Morris Johnson, Lee Foster, and Richard Macon. Pastor Aaron Williams of Tarboro, NC, Pastor Morgan of Momeyer, NC, Evangelists Lorraine Bowman and Phyllis Little, Evangelist Annette Jacobs of Raleigh, NC, Evangelist Bunch of Raleigh, Deacon James Ward and Pastor Davis of Durham, NC. I definitely thank God for my Bible College teachers, Mother Wilma Miles and her son Dr. Russell Miles, who imparted so much of their knowledge of the Word of God to me.

Rise Again

These men and women really poured out the word of God to us, just like they were getting paid for it, that is what impressed me the most about them. The Lord blessed me to connect with some more great men and women of God after I got out of prison, such as Pastor Mike Bullock, and his lovely wife, Evangelist Edith Bullock, people who love God and God's people. Pastor Joe Ferguson, a man who truly has a heart for God, God's people, and the things of God, and Evangelist Shirley Faulks, a truly anointed woman of God, who was just like a mother to my oldest son, the late Prophet D. "Doc" Taylor.

I spent a total of 34 months of a possible 40 months sentence in prison. The last 24 months were spent at Bunn prison. The Lord answered many of my prayer petitions while I was at Bunn. I would write down my petitions and put them in my Bible on Jeremiah 33:3 where it says, "Call to me, and I will answer you, and show you great and mighty things which you do not know".

Some of the prayers were answered. One was my prayer for God to save my marriage, in which He did. I prayed for my wife to be delivered form smoking cigarettes, gambling and playing bingo, and he did; and I prayed that my son, Jermaine would be released early form prison, and he got out one year earlier than he was scheduled to be released. I know that I am not all that I should be, but I thank God I am not who I used to be, but I love the man of God that I am becoming in Jesus Christ. The Lord took my mess, and gave me a message, which became ministry. Today, I help a couple of our deacons to teach Bible study at Louisburg College on Tuesday nights, Deacon Mike Taylor and Deacon Lee Foster. I also witness on the streets of Louisburg and Bunn NC, every chance I get. I love telling others what God has done for me. I know one thing, I don't wish a heroin addiction on my worst enemy. I praise God today that I am truly delivered. You see true deliverance is taking control of what once had control of you. I know that the Word of God is what set me free, because I began speaking God's Word daily, about being healed and delivered. The more word you have in you, the more power you have. The word is what keeps you and sustains you. Also where the Spirit of the Lord is, there is liberty.

Each and every day, my soul seeks to please God!! Praise God!!

Chapter 13

DEVOTIONS

DEVOTIONS I SHARED WITH THE OFFICERS AND INMATES AT BUNN PRISON

PRAYER OF COMMTTMENT TO GOD

Lord, I present myself unto You. May Your will be done in my life. May I never forget that I have surrendered all I am to You. I commit myself to be one whom You can use, consecrated and separated unto Your purposes. I'll pay the price by denying the flesh. If you call me in the night time, I'll get on my knees and pray. If I am never seen of men, and if I always work behind the scenes, still I will be faithful. I lay aside all personal ambition. I'll be one who walks in the spirit and in Your perfect will. Your will shall be wrought in my heart, in my life and in my ministry, in Jesus name, Amen!

PRAYER OF PRAISE

Heavenly Father, I pray that You would help me to establish a new lifestyle, a lifestyle of praise and true worship unto you. Thank You, Father, because I know You have heard and answered all of my petitions. Now by faith, I'm going to praise You for every answer. Father, it is my earnest desire to let your praise continually flow from my lips, in Jesus name, Amen!!!

PRAYER OF SALVATION

Dear Lord, I am a sinner. I ask you to come into my heart, forgive my sins and be my Lord and my Savior. I believe you died for me, and God raised you from the dead, and now you sit on the right hand of God, and I thank you for saving me!!! In Jesus name, Amen!

Rise Again

Dear Lord, I come to You today thanking You for Your loving kindness, I thank you that, even though I have made some wrong decisions in my life which have led me away from You and caused me to be unfaithful, Your faith still abides in me and You still love me.

Though my fellowship has been broken with you, Jesus is still my Lord and Savior. I am sorry for all of my sins. I am tired of living in remorse for what I have done, and I repent of my sins and ask your forgiveness. I thank You that Your forgiveness and mercy do not depend on my good works, but are available to me simply through your grace. I am so glad your mercy endures forever and is new every morning. I make a whole-hearted commitment to you and your word this day. Help me to take one day at a time, trusting your grace and mercy to see me through every moment. Thank You, God, for restoration of our fellowship and for giving me back my joy as your child, In Jesus name, Amen!!!

Rise Again

PRIORITIES ....(I ASKED GOD)

I Asked God to grant me patience, God said no, patience is a by-product of tribulations, it isn't granted, it is earned.

I asked God to give me happiness, God said no, I give you blessings, happiness is up to you.

I asked God to spare me pain, God said no, suffering draws you apart from worldly cares and brings you closer to me.

I asked God to make my spirit grow, God said, no, You must grow on your own, but I will prune you to make you fruitful.

I asked God for all things that I might enjoy in life, God said no, I will give you life so that you may enjoy all things.

I asked God to help me love others, as much as He loves me, God said…AHHH, finally you have the idea .

Here are some of the scriptures that I would share with them.

Jeremiah 29:11-14, For I know the thoughts that I think toward you, says the Lord, thoughts of peace, and not evil, to give you a future and a hope!

V12. Then you will call to me, and go and pray to me, and I will listen to you.

V13. And you will seek me and find me, when you search for me with all of your heart.

V14. I will be found by you, says the Lord, and I will bring you back from your captivity. I will gather you from all the nations, and all the places where I have driven you, says the Lord, and I will bring you back to the place from which I caused you to be carried away captive.

Rise Again

Isaiah 1:19, 20, If you are willing and obedient, you shall eat the good of the land; V:20, But if you refuse and rebel, You shall be devoured by the sword, For the mouth of Lord has spoken!

II Chronicles 7:14, If my people who are called by my name will humble themselves, and pray and seek my face, and turn from their wicked ways, then I will hear from heaven, and forgive their sin and heal their land!

Matthew 4:4, But He answered and said, it is written, man shall not live by bread alone, but by every word that proceeds from the mouth of God!

John 3:3, Jesus answered and said to him most assuredly, I say to you, unless one is born again, he cannot see the kingdom of God!

John 3:16, For God so loved the world that He gave His only begotten Son, that whoever believes in Him should not perish, but have everlasting life!

Philippians 4:13, I can do all things through Christ who strengthens me!

Proverbs 3:5, 6, trust in the Lord with all your heart, and lean not on your own understanding, In all your ways acknowledge Him, and He shall direct your paths.

Psalm 11:25, The generous soul will be made rich, and he who waters will also be watered himself.

Psalm 11:30, The fruit of the righteous is a tree of life, and he who wins souls is wise.

Rise Again

Where to find comfort and encouragement in the Psalms

a. When you feel abandoned-Psalm 10

b. When your world seems to be falling apart-Psalm 46

c. When you are afraid- Psalm 23, 91

d. When you feel guilty- Psalm 51

e. When your family gets on your nerves-Psalm 127,128

f. When you are facing a great challenge- Psalm 27

g. When you see the wicked prospering-Psalm 37, 73

h. When you do not feel very thankful- Psalm 107

i. When you feel God has forgotten you- Psalm 139

j. When you are tempted to lose faith in God-Psalm 62

k. When you have lost your eternal perspective- Psalm 90

l. When you feel like you are barely holding on -Psalm 86

m. When you are wondering what God expects- Psalm 15

n. When you want to know God better- Psalm 42, 63

o. When you need to be reminded of the goodness of God -Ps103

p. When you need to recommit yourself to God- Psalm 116

q. When you need wisdom- Psalm 119

r. When you need a reminder of God's mercy- Psalm 136

s. When you feel like celebrating- Psalm 95-100

Chapter 14

TRANSFORMATION

Before I got out of prison on Sept.7, 2006, I set these goals and plans.

* The first goal I set was to find me a good church home, that preaches and teaches the whole Bible, and where the anointing of God is present. After visiting about 3 churches, my wife and I both agreed that Freedom and Deliverance Outreach center was the best place for us. I loved the way that Bishop Lorenzo Peterson preached and taught the word of God, but it was the love of the church family that sealed the deal.

* The second goal I had set, was to start my own business, and on Nov. 28, 2006, the Lord blessed me to start my courier's service. I signed an Independent Contractor contract with American Expedite Courier services, and would sub-contract work from them. I was blessed with a 2006 cargo van, with only 22,000 miles on it, the same day I had signed my first courier contract.

*The third goal I had set was to go to Bible College to learn more about the Bible, and to complete the 2 year course, and hopefully get my minister's license, because I know I was called by God to preach and teach his word. On May 30, 2008, I received my 2 year Bible College Certificate, Alleluia! I felt like Jonah when I first got out of prison, I was in a hurry to be about God's business, because I had procrastinated and been disobedient long enough. I preached my initial sermon on Aug. 9, 2007.

Rise Again

* My fourth goal was to write this book, and I finally got started on it in January, 2009. My wife and I started our own home-based business in Dec. of 2008.

* My fifth goal is to build my wife her dream home, and with God's help that will happen soon, Praise God!

To me the most important thing about goals is having one. The purpose of goals is to focus our attention on them. Our minds will not reach toward achievement until clear objectives are identified. The magic begins when we set goals. It is then that the switch is turned on, the current begins to flow and the power to accomplish becomes a reality.

* My sixth goal is to take my wife on a 4 day and 3 night cruise to the Bahamas, and I am working on that as I write this book, and I know it too, will come to pass, Praise God!!!

Chapter 15

LIFE AFTER BUNN

I truly thank God for resurrecting my life, my marriage, my relationships with my children, grandchildren, my sisters, and other family members, and in-laws. He has placed my feet on solid ground. God blessed me to be connected to some awesome men and women of God. I especially thank Him for connecting me with Jack Darnell, an awesome man of God, who has a heart after God's heart, whom I met while contracting work through Dash Courier Services. Mr. James Ward, another awesome man of God, who also has a heart after God's heart, a deacon at my church. I am glad that God has strengthened the relationships with my sisters, Josette Daniels and Mrs. Judie D. Barnes, two mighty women of God, whom I love dearly.

Josette is the founder and CEO of Maggie and Erma's house in Greensboro, NC. It is a nine month program for single women in recovery, from alcohol and drugs. She started this Christian-based program on June 10, 2002, and she has about an 85% success rate. Judie is an Evangelist who travels all over the world preaching and teaching the Word of God. She has a wonderful husband, 1st Sgt. Marty Barnes, who supports her whole heartedly. He is the best brother-in law that anyone could have. The Lord has blessed him to survive 3 tours of duty in Iraq. He is hoping to retire from the Army in the summer of 2009.

I thank God for my 4 aunts, Aunt Laura Chance, of Brooklyn, NY, a mighty woman of God, Aunt Ida Mae Hicks of Buffalo, NY, a loving and caring woman of God, Aunt Martha Chapman, of Greenville, NC, a loving and caring woman of God, Aunt Annie L. Hubbard of Greenville, NC, who is also loving and caring woman of God. I thank God for my 2 uncles, Mr. Joe Louis Daniels of Scotland Neck, NC, and Mr. William M. Daniels, of Baltimore, MD, who always kept me in check, whenever I would get out of line, and would remind me to be secure in who I was. I was truly blessed on both sides of my family tree, the Daniels side, which is my Father's side, and the Teel side, which is my Mother's side.

I truly feel like prison was exactly what I needed to change me into the man of God that I am today. I had to be broken, because I was too hard headed, rebellious, selfish, rude, disrespectful, impatient, self-centered, and hard to get along with. Those 34 months did me a lot of good! Now God is teaching me that my Salvation experience does not make me act any better than I ever did. I must renew my mind daily with the Word of God, and spend time with the Holy Spirit. I have got to be plugged into the Spirit of the Living God. I have come to find out that it is possible to hear the Word, read the word, and even teach the work, and still remain unchanged and unaffected. All scripture will teach us, convict us, enrich us, heal us, warn us, and expose our hearts. But we have to act on God's word. That is why the word tells us to be doers of the word, and not hearers only deceiving yourselves as stated in James 1:22!

We have to ask God to speak to us every time we read his word, and show us what we should be doing in response to it. As Christians, we should stand out like a sparkling diamond against a rough background. You should be more wholesome than anyone else. We should be firm in the things that we do and don't do, and refuse to allow the world to pull us down to its level! Alleluia!

In December of 2007, I received news that my oldest son, the late Prophet, D. "Doc" Taylor, did not have long to live. It really tore my heart up, because he was only 31 years old, and I thought he was in the prime of his preaching ministry. I prayed and asked God, to help me to accept whatever His will was for my son. God also revealed to me, that I cannot become too attached to anyone or anything down here on earth, other than Him, that I cannot let go of. He truly gave me a peace that surpassed all understanding. On Feb. 3, 2008 the Lord took my son home to be with Him. Then at his home-going service, we truly celebrated his life, and praised God for the wonderful 31 years of his life. Even though my son had flaws and weaknesses, he was an awesome young man of God. I never met a young man of his age that possessed the Revelation knowledge, wisdom, and understanding of God's Word, and break it down so good that even a baby 5 years old could understand it. He was truly anointed and appointed by God, for such a time as this. He will be truly missed by all that ever knew him. Then too, death is but a gain of glory, for those that are in Jesus Christ. I still say today, that God is a good God, and He's good all the time. He is in control of everything. He is my source, and He has many resources by which to bless you with, to help you, and to provide for you.

God uses our setbacks in life to move us forward. Through my toughest storms, God has proven to be Faithful; He has restored my Hope, strengthened my Faith, and renewed my love relationship with Him. I am convinced that we should live to give, and we should ask the Lord every day to show us how we can share His love with others by giving of our time, talents, and resources. You make a living out of what you get; you make a life out of what you give. As Christians, we must watch our thoughts because they become our words, watch our words, because they become our habits, we must watch our habits, because they become our behavior and character. We should start looking forward to our eternal home that God has prepared for his children. We must continue to be faithful to God here on earth, and help as many as we can to come to know Jesus while we are here on earth!

Today, I know what it feels like to be set free. I have been clean for over 5 years now, and I am walking in my deliverance each and every day. One of the songs that I keep on my heart is, "I am free, Praise the Lord. I am free, no longer bound, no more chains holding me, my soul is resting, it is such a blessing, praise the Lord. Alleluia, I am Free!!" I am reminded of Jesus' words in Luke 22:31,32 "And the Lord said, Simon, Simon, indeed, Satan has asked for you, that he may sift you as wheat, But I have prayed for you, that your faith should not fail, and when you have returned to me, strengthen your brethren." Now I am on a

Rise Again

mission to win as many souls as I can to Jesus Christ, and to let my brothers and sisters know that he or she whose hope is in God, is not hopeless. If they are not satisfied with the direction their life is going, they can change it today with God's help. Jesus did it for me, and He will certainly do it for them. There is nothing too hard for God, or impossible for Him to do. Only the humble gets the help, so let that pride go. When I think back over my life, and I see where God has brought me from, what He has brought me through, and where He has brought me to, that is why I say, it makes me wanna Shout! Alleluia! I am determined to go all the way with Jesus, and see what the end is gonna be. The end of a thing is better than the beginning. A small beginning is just a prelude to a great finale!

Never let your current circumstances dictate the vision of your Future!

Rise Again

WASTED TIME

The time I've wasted is my worse regret,
much spent in places I can never forget.
Often I think about things I have done --
the tears, the laughter, the hurt, and the fun.

Woe unto me for my sorrows and guilt
and the walls of doubt I should not have built.
I'm trapped in my body wanting to run
back to my youth where it had all begun.

The chase is over with no place to hide
I have nothing left, not even my pride.
As reality hits me square in the face,
I'm scared, alone, a prisoner to this place.

As memories of the past flash in my head,
the tracks of my tears show the pain I've had.
I ask myself why and where I went wrong:
I guess I was weak when I should've been strong.

Living for the drugs and the wings I'd grown
I was a hostage and left all alone.
As I look at my past, it's easy to see
I was most afraid of being poor me.

I pretended to be hard, fast, and cool
all I was really was a mixed up fool.
I've gotten too old for this tiresome game
without a conscience or a sense of shame.

It's time that I change and get on with life
providing for my children and my wife.
What my future holds, I really don't know,
but the years I've lost have begun to show.
I've lived with the hope I'd get a new start
because I still hold dreams deep in my heart.
I hope I can make it, at least I will try,

Rise Again

'cause death is ahead, and it's too soon to die.
-AUTHOR UNKNOWN

P.S. Your life is God's Gift to You

What you do with your life is your Gift back to God!!!!

John 3:16 For God so loved the world that he gave his only

Begotten son, that whoever believes in him

Should not perish but have Everlasting Life!!!!

J. C.'s Quotations

Power Points that I would share during Bible Study in prison!

Our greatest glory consists not, of never falling, but of rising every time we fall.

It is better to be prepared, and not get the opportunity, than to get the opportunity, and not be prepared.

You don't need to be big to think big thoughts. You need to think big thoughts to become big. This is the faith in vision.

God takes us the routes He does in life to get us to our vision, so that we can develop character and become more responsible.

A life not lived for others is not worth living!

The poorest person in the world is not the man or woman without a nickel; it is the man or woman without a dream.

It is never too late to become what you might have been.

Who you are speaks so loudly that people cannot hear what you are saying, because they are looking at your walk and not listening to your talk.

It is not what you do occasionally that makes you who you are but what you do consistently.

Stop telling God how big your storm is, instead tell your storm how big God is!

In dark moments, seek God; in quiet moments, Hear God; In fearful moments, Trust God, He's moving Your Way!!

Words Of Inspiration and Encouragement

Each of us was conceived by destiny, produced by purpose, and packaged with potential to live a meaningful and fulfilling life.

Your past is behind you. Do not seek to recapture what is now history. Your power is in your destiny, make the necessary adjustments for where you are now in life. Maintain your focus, my brothers, my sisters, and for God's sake, keep moving forward!

Remember, you were created to stand out not blend in. You were designed not only to be special and unique, but also to specialize. You were created to accomplish something that no one else can accomplish!

Your cross in life is all of your spiritual tests, afflictions, burdens, and oppositions in life!

There is a reason that you are who you are. But there is an even greater purpose for your life. You may be who you are, but you are not yet who you will be.
God has bigger and better things ahead for you. Each one of us is called to be partakers of the glory that is yet to be revealed.

God takes His time about bringing us our full deliverance. He uses the difficult times to stretch our Faith, and let patience have its perfect work. God's timing is Perfect!

Christian courage is the willingness to say and do the right thing regardless of earthly cost, because God promises to help you and save you on account of Jesus Christ!

Final Thoughts

Drug abuse and alcoholism destroys your ability to live a responsive life. It is a form of self-destruction. It's not just the drugs or alcohol, but it's the negative attitudes and bad behaviors that come along with these addictions.

Keeping up with personal hygiene is one thing that most addicts feel they can do without. Their top priority is to get high.

Most people turn to drugs or alcohol because they have been scarred emotionally because their hopes and dreams have been shattered; such was the case for me.

I could not deal with rejection after my failed professional baseball career. I began to feel like there was no hope for me in life, and I developed a "don't care" attitude. But I thank God for a praying mother, who stood on Joshua 24:15; "Choose ye this day whom you shall serve, but as for me and my house we shall serve the Lord." I thank God for a praying grandmother and other family members too! Like a light bulb turning on one day, I was reading a book by T.D. Jakes and it became clear. The book read "He or she whose hope is in God is not hopeless. So I cried out to God for myself and he heard my cry and saved and delivered me. Today, my desire is to reach back and help as many as possible to come to know the Lord Jesus Christ and let them know that they can surely "Rise Again".

For me, it took me to surrender every area of my life to Jesus Christ and to allow Him to deliver me and change me.

Rise Again

In Memory of

Jessie L. Daniels
(Father)
April 2, 1934 –
February 13, 1995

Erma L. Daniels
(Mother)
September 25, 1935 –
April 15, 1985

Reverend D. Doc Taylor (My Eldest Son)
April 15, 1976 – February 3, 2008

Rise Again

In Memory of

Jeffery M. Daniels (Brother)
June 5, 1956 – November 20, 2006

Blenda Gay (Cousin)
November 22, 1950 – December 20, 1976

Reflections of Me

LOUISBURG COLLEG BASEBALL TEAM

FRANKLIN TIMES NEWSPAPER JAN. 1977
Dodgers Pick J.C. Daniels

The Los Angeles Dodgers picked Louisburg's second baseman, J.C. Daniels, in the second round of last week's major league draft. Daniels, a sophomore, led the North Carolina Collegiate League this summer in hitting with a .369 average and in homeruns with 11. "Without a doubt, J.C. is one of the best players we have had here at Louisburg," commented Coach Russ Frasier. "He has all the tools it takes to play professional baseball, and I expect him to go a long way before he is through. One of his chief assets is his desire to play, and in most cases this makes all the difference in the world." Daniels is expected to sign with the Dodgers after the Hurricanes complete their coming season.

Rise Again

Reflections of Me

1977 Los Angeles Dodgers Picks in the MLB January Draft-Regular Phase

Drafted Players

Year	Rnd	DT	OvPck	RdPck	Tm	Pos	WAR	G	AB	HR	BA	OPS	G	W	L	ERA	WHIP	SV	Type	Drafted Out of
1977	1	1rg	19	19	Dodgers	Tim Gloyd	SS												JC	Sacramento City College (Sacramento, CA)
1977	2	1rg	45	19	Dodgers	Jessie Daniels	2B												JC	Louisburg College (Louisburg, NC)
1977	3	1rg	71	19	Dodgers	Rocky Cordova	RHP												JC	Sacramento City College (Sacramento, CA)
1977	4	1rg	96	18	Dodgers	Daniel Forer	LHP												JC	Iowa Western Community College (Council Bluffs, IA)
1977	5	1rg	118	15	Dodgers	Larry Wright	RHP												JC	Georgia Perimeter College (Covington, GA)
1977	6	1rg	138	15	Dodgers	Ronald Grout	1B												4Yr	Wingate University (Wingate, NC)
1977	7	1rg	155	13	Dodgers	Randall May	RHP												JC	Yakima Valley Community College (Yakima, WA)

Made in the USA
Charleston, SC
04 April 2012